Memories Too Few

A Letter to Parents about Pregnancy Loss

BY Kathy Manning Burns

Memories Too Few

A Letter to Parents about Pregnancy Loss

Kathy Manning Burns

In-Sight Books, Inc
PO Box 42467
Oklahoma City, Oklahoma 73123
800.658.9262 or 405.810.9501
www.insightbooks.com
orders&info@insightbooks.com

Printed and bound in the United States of America

ISBN 1-892785-73-0

Thank you to

The friends who shared their stories with me, Joyce Lung and Lisa Pendleton of Deaconess Hospital PRIDE for their advice, and my sisters, parents and sons who encouraged me to write this book.

3/10

To the Reader

When you lose a child by any pregnancy or newborn loss, unfortunately, the only people on this earth that truly understand your pain are other parents who have experienced the same loss. Others can sympathize but they can not know your pain.

I have been there, I know your pain and I would like to offer you my support.

If you are not feeling a major loss, you should not wonder if there is something wrong with you. If your pregnancy loss came before you had felt an attachment, you may not experience feelings of loss like I describe here. Some people may also experience a delayed reaction to a loss. In either case, just hold on to this book. You may find you want to read it at some later point.

I have written this book as I would write a letter to a friend who had suffered a pregnancy loss, stillbirth or newborn death. If I were really writing a friend, this would be a series of letters or conversations and would be broken up into smaller bites. I encourage you to read this book in the same way. Read the portion that applies to you at the time or read as much as you feel you can take in, then put it down. Pick it up again later when you are ready to go further.

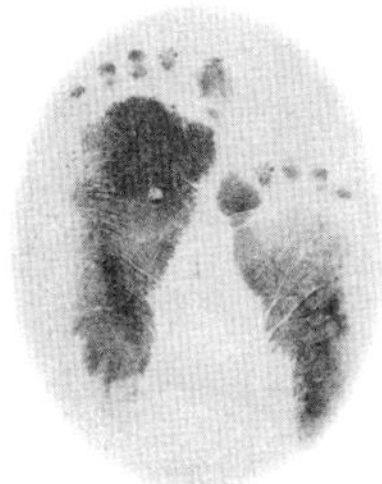

Dedicated to my parents

Doug & Barbara Manning

Their knowledge, wisdom and compassion saw me through the darkness

- Kathy Burns

In Memory of

____

your baby's name

Section I
Beginning the Journey

Dear Grieving Parent,

Your life has been changed. No matter how your baby died—premature birth, miscarriage, stillbirth, as a newborn or from any number of complications—you must now face life without this child. The first thing I want to tell you is, you will survive this pain. Your world has been turned upside down and you may not be sure you can survive it, but you can and I feel privileged to have the opportunity to help you walk through it.

If there were any way I could take this pain away, anything I could do, any words I could say, I would. All I can do is tell you how sorry I am and tell you I have been where you are now. I share my story with you in the hope that it will help you in some small way.

I cannot tell you exactly what your grief will be like. I cannot tell you how long your grief will last. Every person grieves in their own way. Grief is unique to each individual, each personality, each situation. As you read along, if you find something that does not seem to fit you, it doesn't mean you are doing your grief wrong; you can't do it wrong, it is *your* grief. All I can do is tell you what has been observed about grief, stories I have been told and my personal experiences. Not everything will fit you, but I hope you find some nuggets of truth that help.

My son, Isaac, was premature and only lived thirty-four hours. His stay was brief but his impact has been far reaching. I had no idea how much had changed when I left the hospital after he died, I just knew that leaving without a baby in my arms was one of the most painful and difficult things I had ever done. Nothing felt right.

I felt what you are probably feeling now, life had been disrupted and while I longed to be home, I knew home would never be the same again. My world had been forever changed.

Shock, Whirl & Survival

At first I was in shock. You may be too. You may find yourself just moving through the day without any real connection to what is going on around you. I remember things feeling rather surreal. My mind was working and telling me what to do, but the connection between my mind and my feelings had been severed. You may find that you are functioning, taking care of what needs to be done, but at the same time you may feel that you are standing aside, watching things happen.

You may also find that your mind races and it may be very difficult to concentrate. It is in a whirl. You may think of something that needs to be done but before you can act on it, your mind has jumped to another thought and you have totally forgotten what you were thinking about in the first place. You may feel like your mind is spinning out of control.

I don't know that words can properly describe this period of Shock & Whirl. You feel like your mind is firing on all cylinders but at the same time is sluggish. You are totally aware of what is going on but, at the same time, confused. It is almost as if you are watching a movie in fast motion. Everything is moving so quickly and flashing by, but you are standing off to the side watching, just trying to make sense of it all.

In the midst of the Shock & Whirl you may also have moments of dread; times when you ask yourself how you are going to get through this, how are you going to handle this? You look ahead to the time to come and wonder how you will find happiness again. All these questions basically boil down to one question I mentioned at the beginning of this book, "Can I survive this pain?"

Don't panic, the Shock & Whirl period is normal. The questions about surviving are normal. Eventually you will find your equilibrium. The movie that you are watching will slow down and you will be able to keep up. Just take each day at your pace and one day you will realize that your pace and the rest of the world's are in sync again. That day will come.

Beginning the Journey

Your journey through grief began the moment you realized your child would not survive. Here, at the beginning, there is a mix of physical and emotional issues you will need to face.

The Body Betrayal

You will want to discuss with your doctor any physical concerns. Just as any woman who has been through a pregnancy, your body has to adjust to no longer being pregnant. You may have also had surgery or other medical procedures from which you will need to recover. Follow your physician's advice and take care of yourself in order to give yourself time to heal.

Some of your physical care may also be tied closely to your emotional care. A few days after Isaac died my breasts filled and were extremely painful. I followed the medical advice on how to deal with my full breasts. But the physical pain was not the worst part of it for me. I felt betrayed by my body. My mind knew that there was not a baby to feed; why didn't my body know too? It was neither logical nor rational, but it is how I felt. So while I was wrapping myself tightly to deal with the physical problem of engorged breasts, I was sobbing, dealing with the emotional issues of having no child to hold and feed.

The Nursery Dilemma

In the first few days after your loss you may also have other issues to deal with: what to do with the baby's room and things you had prepared for him or her, telling your friends and family about your loss, possibly funeral or memorial plans. You will have your own list.

If you already had a room prepared for the baby, some people close to you may encourage you to let them put everything away so that you will not have to see all those baby items. These people are afraid that seeing the baby things will remind you of your loss. What they don't realize is that you will not have to be reminded of your loss, it will be on your mind every moment. Go with your instincts. If you want the things put away, fine. If you don't, ask your friends to leave them as they are. Do what feels right to you. This is your grief, not anyone else's, so do whatever is healing for you.

I have a friend named Sarah whose mother cleaned out the baby's room and packed everything away while Sarah was still in the hospital, all without a word to her. It was quite an unpleasant shock to her when she returned home. As she put it, "I was not prepared for an empty room along with my empty heart." Facing an empty room was not easier, it was harder. In a way, that empty room symbolized how the family dealt with loss then and to this day. They packed it all away and no one ever spoke about the baby again.

Planning a Service

Deciding whether to have a funeral or memorial service is another area where you need to do what feels right to you.

Many hospitals bury the infants that were lost early in a pregnancy and hold a memorial service twice a year, inviting the families to attend. You also have the option of going through a local funeral home to hold your own service. If your loss was later in the pregnancy, you will most likely deal directly with funeral professionals, depending on the laws in your state.

If the mother's health prevents her from attending a funeral at this time, the family may want to go ahead with burial or cremation now and hold a memorial service later when all can attend. Another option is to ask the funeral home if they are able to hold the baby until the mother is able to attend the funeral.

I would encourage you to hold some kind of service. It could be as simple as your immediate family gathering in the living room to a full service at the funeral home. Have a time to come together with the people who are important in your life and say good-bye. You are not only saying good-bye to your baby, you are saying good-bye to all the hopes and dreams you had for this child. Even if you plan to attend the memorial service offered by your hospital, that service may be months away. Planning and holding a service with your family now could be very helpful and healing. It is the last opportunity you have to do anything tangible for your child, and can help with acceptance and acknowledgement of your loss.

As parents you started bonding and connecting with this baby the moment you knew you were pregnant. You started building your life around this child's needs. You started preparing your family and your home for his or her arrival. You started making plans for the future. Those plans could have been as everyday as planning to play ball in the yard, taking the baby to the park or on a future Disney vacation. You may have even thought as far as college or of playing with this child's children, your grandchildren. Whatever those hopes, plans, dreams were for this child, saying good-bye to them is part of saying good-bye to your baby.

We held a funeral for Isaac. That was what was right for our family and our situation. It was touching that two of Isaac's nurses came, they were some of the very few that had a chance to know Isaac in the few hours he was alive. The funeral or memorial service is an opportunity for your friends and family to show their support for you. It also is a part of establishing the significance of the child you have lost.

Establishing Significance

Establishing significance is an important part of grief. Any time something happens to us we have a need to establish the significance. If you stub your toe, find a great bargain at the store, or lose a favorite piece of jewelry, chances are you can't wait to tell someone about it. Telling our friends and family about both the good and the bad things that happen to us is how we establish the significance of those events in our lives. Some things, of course, are of greater significance than others.

In our society a loss of an infant by miscarriage, stillbirth or newborn is often viewed as minor grief. Conventional wisdom says, "After all, you did not even know the child and had not had a chance to bond with it." Many people do not understand that the bonding process begins long before you are able to hold a child in your arms. This is a significant event in your life. One you will not forget.

An older couple came to visit me after my son died. As we visited I discovered that they had lost a child in similar circumstances nearly sixty years earlier. This couple had three adult children and had lived full lives. Still, they never forgot the child they lost. They called him by name and told me how old he would have been if he had lived. He was significant and an important part of their lives. They also understood, like few other people did, that my grief was not minor and Isaac was significant.

An older man in our church died from complications after surgery shortly after Isaac died. As his wife, Ellen, and I both walked through our grief I noticed an important difference. In the first few weeks after the funeral, Ellen spent time each day going through some of her husband's belongings. She started giving some items away to people she knew would appreciate them. Other items she began placing aside for a future auction. There were some things she kept for herself, of course, but she was spending time dispersing things.

For Ellen, establishing the significance of her husband meant sharing a part of him with those around her. She had so many years worth of items that he had owned and collected that she could share these with friends and loved ones. In that act, she could say that her husband had been important and had many friends who would value having something of his.

On the other hand, I had so few things that were Isaac's that I bought a plastic storage bin so I could preserve every item. I had all the sympathy cards my family had received, I had the little construction paper stocking with Isaac's name on it and other adornments that the nurses had decorated Isaac's bassinet with in the hospital. I had the very few pictures of Isaac both before and after his death. We bought a doll so that we could use its clothes to bury Isaac in and I kept that doll. I even bought a duplicate blanket just like the one I had tucked in around Isaac in his casket so I would have another reminder of him.

Establishing significance for me had a different kind of urgency than it did for Ellen; for her it meant dispersing, for me establishing significance meant gathering in.

As time went on, my family found other ways to establish significance. We took great pains to pick out just the right stone and come up with just the right design for his grave marker. We brought flowers to his grave at holidays. We would make donations in memory of him. Even writing this book is in some measure an act of establishing significance.

You will need to find ways to establish the significance of your loss. How you do that will be unique to you. It does not have to be anything forced or artificial. It may be something public or it may be more personal and private. Each time you tell the story of what has happened to you, you are establishing the significance of a child that you longed to have. Each time you light a candle and say your child's name, you are establishing significance. Even the act of giving your child a name establishes significance.

Those who have not lost an infant in this way may not understand your need. They may not realize what an impact this will have on your life. But, you know that whether you were able to hold your baby or not, whether you were able to look into his eyes or not, whether you were able to bring her home from the hospital and lay her down to sleep in the crib or not, this little person was a member of your family. The bond and connection began forming from the moment you first learned you were expecting a child. Honoring that bond and the hopes and dreams you had for this particular child helps you, so do whatever you need to establish the significance of this longed for child.

Continuing the Journey

Immediately after your loss, your friends and family will be there, they will offer many words of sympathy and offer help and support. They can be a great help to you. However, after a couple of weeks, many will return to their normal routines and may not be as present for you as they were in the beginning. This is partly because many people assume that grief only lasts about two weeks. Those who have not been through grief have no idea of the time needed to work through it.

Words of Comfort?

At the beginning of your third week after your loss your journey through grief is not coming to an end but has just begun. Along the way you will find there are many things that people say or do that help and many that do not.

We assume that our friends and family will be the ones to really come through for us during a crisis. Sometimes this is true but sometimes these same people can, in their efforts to provide comfort, say things that really hurt. I think many times our friends don't think through what they are saying, they may just be repeating clichés they have heard before.

In truth, when faced with a person in grief, people tend to panic. They suddenly feel that they have to come up with something to say that will make you feel better, make you stop crying, or somehow make you recover from your grief in an instant. They may have the best intentions at heart, and will spout something out that they think is profound but actually hurts and sometimes makes you angry. I have several examples.

I have a friend who was told she was "one of the fortunate ones, she would have a baby to rock in heaven." Now, truly, how bizarre is it to tell a grieving parent that they are fortunate?

After my son died, a lovely older lady actually said to me that it should give me comfort to know that, "Isaac is in heaven. There is no telling what he would have grown up to be and whether he would have gone to heaven. But now, you know he is in heaven." Once again, statements like this are another message to a grieving parent that they are fortunate. Why would you tell someone who just suffered a loss that they are fortunate?

Then there is another friend who had someone tell her that she "was one of the few strong enough to go through such an ordeal." I like to think that I am a strong, capable woman. But, this is a time when no matter how strong you are, you need someone to lean on and to be present for you to lend you their strength. Statements like this can make you feel pressured to put on a good face and not show the world how much you are hurting. This is not a time when you should feel you have to be strong in order to make others feel better. This is their time to be strong for you.

An older man, a veteran, grabbed me one day several weeks after Isaac had died, and told me a long story about how he had been shot during the war, but when he got up he realized that the bullet had not touched him because it had been stopped by the Bible in his shirt pocket. He ended his story with, "When it's your time to go, it's your time to go." I am still at a loss to try and figure out how that was supposed to help. It was obvious that he thought he had done me a great service; he had given me a "new way to think about my loss" and had a satisfied grin on his face at offering this help.

If you are a church goer, you may be expecting that you will find the most comfort among your fellow church members. Unfortunately, most church members are just as clueless about what to say, but feel compelled to say something. You may hear, "All things work together for good." My personal favorite is, "God will not put any more on you than you can bear." Ugh! That one really makes me angry. Our friends at church may have the best of intentions, but most of them, like the rest of our society, just do not know what to say or do. They hope that saying something that sounds holy will be the key to curing your grief. However, most of the scriptures people believe will provide comfort at this time tend to fall short. Often, they choose scripture that gives the impression that your pain is not that great. Telling you your pain is not that bad is not what helps. Perhaps the best verse a grieving parent can hang on to is John 11:35 "Jesus wept."

You may ask why people say these things? There is a misconception in our society that all someone who is sad needs is a new way to think about it. If they can give you a reason to understand your loss, they will have made your grief disappear and made you happy again. We have a fear of grief and generally see it as our mission to eradicate it as quickly as possible. So, by helping you see the silver lining of your dark cloud, they believe they are helping you.

You, too, may face these well-meaning friends. It is up to you as to how you handle them. You can grin and bear it or you can tell them they don't know what they're talking about. You can hand them this book and tell them not to talk to you until after they have read it or you can go find other friends for a while. However you choose to handle it is up to you. Just remember that grief is not something to stuff inside and never let out. There may be times you have to put on a good face but be sure to find someone you can cry with, someone who knows clichés and so called *words of comfort* don't work.

Mr. Cellophane

Cellophane, Mr. Cellophane should have been
my name, Mr. Cellophane.
'Cause you can look right through me, Walk right by me,
And never know I'm there.

Those are words from the song *Mr. Cellophane,* from the 1975 stage musical and 2002 movie, *Chicago.* They can be used to describe a certain dimension of the grieving process.

Grief can make you feel like a Mr. Cellophane. For several days, or even a couple of weeks, after your loss, people express their sympathy, and send cards or flowers. Some may even bring meals in. However, there comes a point when everyone else returns to their lives and busy schedules and you are left to cope on your own. That is when you feel like Mr. Cellophane.

You go to the grocery store, the mall, to work, or wherever there are people, and it seems to you that your grief is like a huge neon sign announcing to the world that you are hurting, that you are in pain. It seems that there is no way they could possibly miss seeing this sign—it is flashing bright lights all around with the message PAIN, PAIN, PAIN!

But, no one sees the sign, no one notices, they just walk right by and never know the pain is there.

I had never noticed how many commercials promoting baby products there are—diapers, formula, wipes, etc.—until my son died. I never noticed how many people at the mall were pushing strollers until my son died. I never noticed how many people we come into contact with as we go about our daily lives who know nothing about us, until my son died.

My friend, Sarah, lost her baby, John, to stillbirth nearly 30 years ago right before Thanksgiving. Her family had the funeral for John while she was still in the hospital. Once Sarah came home from the hospital, no one ever said a word to her about John. Every year the family gathers for Thanksgiving, no one mentions John. When the rest of the family shares their blessings, Sarah is thinking of John. While the rest of the family looks forward to the yearly gathering around the table, Sarah detests it. Sarah has been locked in a prison of silence for nearly 30 years. Like Mr. Cellophane, Sarah's family is walking right by her and her pain, never realizing it is there.

Being in grief can be such a lonely time. Even among friends and family you may feel lonely and somehow separate. Sports, shopping, movies, those things that you may have enjoyed before, now seem trivial and unimportant. You watch others get excited and involved in these activities and don't understand how they can be so happy when you are in so much pain. Don't they see it?

There are no quick and easy answers in grief and there is always a "loneliness factor" to it. But, there are some things that do help.

What Helps?

So if clichés and words of comfort don't work, what does? Is there anything someone can say to you that helps? And, if you feel like Mr. Cellophane, is there anything that can help you feel like the world is not passing you by without a glance? Yes and no.

I had three friends who saw me through the darkest times. Nothing they said made me feel better. They had no words of wisdom and they never found a magic spell of just the right words to take my pain away. These friends actually had very little to say at all.

The first friend made a simple gesture that touched my heart. Her name was Barbara, she was one of the ladies providing a meal for my family after the funeral, and she wore a footprints lapel pin. After the meal, Barbara gave me a hug, she did not say much but she did do something unexpected. She took her lapel pin off of her blouse and pinned it onto mine. I know she wore the pin as a reminder of the poem *Footprints in the Sand* which is a beautiful, touching poem. However, to me, the footprints reminded me of Isaac's tiny feet. I wore that pin every single day for at least the first year after Isaac died. I even bought more pins just to be sure I had one in case one got lost or ruined in the laundry. Wearing those footprints near my heart was a daily reminder of Isaac and symbolic of the loss that I felt and in some way enabled me to carry Isaac with me everywhere I went. Only a couple of people knew why I wore that pin every day. I did not need anyone to know. It was my way of remembering my son and his tiny footprints, and it felt like a daily hug from Barbara.

Another friend, Debbie, had lost three babies to miscarriage. She knew my pain in a way that few others could. I don't remember a word Debbie said to me. But, she met me for lunch once a week for months. Debbie let me tell her the same story about losing Isaac over and over again. She let me vent my frustrations and sorrows over and over again. Debbie listened to me describe every event, every emotion, every thought I had and then she listened to me describe them all over again. Not once did she indicate that it was time for me to move on and get over it. Not once did she ever indicate that she was tired of hearing the same thing over and over again. Not once did Debbie use a cliché on me. She shared her story with me and we talked for hours.

Tammy is a true treasure who has wisdom beyond her years and she is an unwavering source of support. She made it a point to mention Isaac by name. I don't know how she knew that would help, that I longed to hear his name, but she knew and wasn't afraid to say it. Tammy also listened. She heard the same stories Debbie did, because that was the only thing on my mind. Tammy listened and never once complained or acted like she did not want to be near me. When I had exhausted everyone else's ears and could tell that they did not want to hear about Isaac anymore, Debbie and Tammy continued to listen.

The Three H's

What helped? Doug Manning says that people in grief need the three H's. They need you to "Hang Around, Hug them, and Hush." That's exactly what my friends did for me. They hung around long past when others had gone on about their business. They hugged me or held my hand and gave me the human touch I needed. And they hushed. They knew that there were no words they could say that could cure me. The only words that would help were mine; telling my story over and over again, explaining my feelings over and over again, that helped.

You need to find friends that can do that for you. You may already have friends that will fill this role for you. If not, go find them. Your local hospital may have a support group or there may be a Compassionate Friends meeting near you. There are also grief chat rooms or forums online which you can join at no charge. You do need to be careful that you find people who can help you in a healthy way. Don't fall for any quick fix cures or promises. Grief must be walked through. It is a long, painful journey. The only way to come out on the other side a healthy, whole being is to walk through it.

Some people prefer to go to a counselor. You must find what works for you. The important thing is to find someone you can tell your story to over and over again until the day comes that you are done talking. You will know it when it comes, don't try to force it, just keep talking until that day arrives.

It is hard to believe that there used to be a day when you may have walked right by someone in pain and did not stop to take notice, to say how sorry you were. There may have been a day when you did not know how to act around someone in grief. Perhaps you tried to pretend everything was normal so you didn't have to deal with those uncomfortable feelings or come up with the right words to say.

Your friends and family may not know how to react to you. They may actually notice the pain but don't know how to respond to it. This grief is one of the loneliest of all. Others may be very sad that your baby is gone but, in the end, they did not know your baby. There are no stories to share about your child that begin with the words, "Remember when..." They had not had the chance to bond with your child as you had.

Fortunately, we have learned some things about grief in the last 30 years. One thing we have learned is that ignoring the pain does not make it go away; pretending like everything is fine does not help. We have also learned that losing a baby does not cause less grief than losing an older child. And we have learned that parents who lose babies need to talk about their loss.

If your family does not know how to bring it up, it is okay for you to do so. Talk about your baby, say his/her name. Friends and family will generally take their cues from you. By mentioning the baby, you send a message to others that it is okay to talk about him/her. Many have the mistaken impression that talking about the baby will "remind" you of your loss. They do not realize that there is not a moment that goes by that you are not thinking about him/her. There is no way they can remind you of something you are already thinking about.

Sarah said that she had friends with small babies who would leave the room whenever she walked in. In their efforts to protect Sarah's feelings, her friends were leaving her feeling lonelier than ever. It is enough to lose your child, you should not have to lose your friends too.

It may be hard, but you may have to tell your loved ones what you need from them. We would like to think that they can just tell by looking at us what we need. Unfortunately, humans are not blessed with mind reading capabilities. Tell them that it is okay to say the baby's name, tell them it is okay to talk about the loss. Tell them that you do not want them to leave the room.

Also be aware that you may be the one blocking interaction. Sarah remembers that her mother did try a few times to talk to her, but Sarah kept changing the subject. She is the one who would not speak about it. It may be difficult to talk about, but find some way to share your feelings with someone. If you find it difficult to speak, it may help to write instead. Write someone you feel comfortable with a letter or correspond by e-mail. Find some way to communicate what you feel.

Yes, there will be awkward moments. Yes, some of the people you love will not be able to handle it in the way you hope. Yes, sometimes you will feel like Mr. Cellophane. But, sometimes, you will be able to mention the loss and relieve the tension in the air and move on. As long as the tension is there, there is no way to move on. The other choice is to be locked in a prison of silence with a life sentence. So take the risk, get your child's name into the room and break out of the prison.

One Foot In Front of the Other

You will often hear people say that they made it through difficult times by taking it one day at a time, or by putting one foot in front of the other. In other words, they did not try to take on the enormity of their situation all at once, but faced their difficulty a small bit at a time. Instead of trying to face your grief all at once, face it in small steps. So, how do you accomplish this? How do you just put one foot in front of the other? It may help to know what to expect in grief.

Waves and Time

We discussed the Shock and Whirl of grief at the beginning of this book. After the first couple of weeks of your grief, as the period of Shock and Whirl is subsiding, you may begin to think that the worst is over. I wish I could tell you that it will all be over soon. But, the truth is, that grief comes in waves and lasts much longer than a few weeks, it may take a couple of years to work through it. That does not mean you will hurt like you hurt now for that long. You will experience ebbs and flows, just like the ocean, as well as periods of calm and storms. These waves of emotion will eventually settle into a more even state and though you may still have some waves of emotion from time to time, they will not be as strong and will not overwhelm you.

If it takes less time does that mean you did not love your child enough? If it takes more does that mean you are weak? No, grief may follow a general pattern, but in the end, it is quite unique. Your grief will follow whatever pattern fits you. What is important is that you allow yourself whatever time you need.

During this time, whatever length of time it is, you may experience your grief in a variety of ways. You may have nightmares or you may want to sleep more than usual, you may feel agitated and impatient at times, or distant with little emotion.

You will also feel anger.

Anger

Anger will present itself in many ways. The anger may be turned inward on yourself or outward toward others. Anger is normal in grief and how you handle that anger is important.

You may not even realize you are angry at first and then suddenly you are just about as mad as you have ever been. Anger is not a bad thing. Actually, anger can give us the strength to claw our way out of the depths of despair. Being angry is not anything to be concerned about. Where anger focuses is of some concern.

Anger may focus on friends or coworkers. When you are in grief, your emotions are raw. It is very easy to take offense at even simple statements. Someone may greet you with, "good morning" and you want to bite their head off. Things that would not have mattered greatly to you before can now become sources of major conflict. It may help to recognize the source of that anger as you deal with the people around you.

Anger may focus on the baby's other parent whether that is a spouse, significant other or partner. This can put a strain on the relationship. Men and women experience grief in different ways and on their own unique schedules. Couples may find themselves fighting more and feeling less connected. It may help to discuss your anger openly and recognize that the source of your anger is your loss, not necessarily anything your partner did or did not do. Recognize that this anger is temporary and with time you hopefully will feel close as a couple again.

Anger may focus on other people with babies or on those who have babies and mistreat them. You may question why the teenager who had a child and threw it in the trash was able to have a child but you weren't. In anger you may ask, "Why me?"

Anger may focus on the doctor or hospital that cared for you during your pregnancy. It may focus on your pastor or congregation or on God. Wherever your anger focuses is okay unless it focuses on you.

There is no way to get around the fact that most of us who lose a baby feel guilt. Just the fact that this life was dependent on you for its survival naturally leads to a feeling of somehow not living up to your responsibility when your child dies.

My friend, Vickie, felt guilty because she was so physically exhausted during the birth that she could not do what the doctor asked her to do. Another friend read that poor dental health can cause premature birth and decided that, since she had not been to a dentist in several years, the loss was her fault.

The list of reasons for feeling guilt goes on and on. The problem with guilt is that it is anger focused on yourself and can be very destructive if allowed to fester. You can find yourself stuck in your grief and going around and around in circles. You must break that cycle in order to move on. You need to find a way to forgive yourself and let go of the guilt. Learn from the experience but do not allow it to destroy you.

Wherever your anger focuses, dealing with it and expressing it can help you move past it. Do not swallow it; find avenues to deal with it. You can do so in a variety of ways: talk about it with a friend you feel safe with, write about it in a journal, or blow off steam in a physical way. I have heard of someone buying dishes at garage sales and then smashing them. Exercise or hit a punching bag. Find something that helps you to release the anger in a healthy way.

The Firsts

The attacks on September 11, 2001 changed our country's focus. Have you noticed how we now refer to and judge everything by whether it happened before or after 9/11? Isaac's death changed me in a way that I can never go back to being exactly who I was before. For me Christmas 1994 is my date, my "before or after Isaac". The date of your baby's death will now become that focus for you.

This will be most obvious to you during the first year of your grief. All the firsts will be challenges and will most likely bring on new waves of grief. The firsts may include:

The first time you go to work after your loss.
The first time you go to church after your loss.
The first time you see a particular friend after your loss.
The first time you go to a movie after your loss.
The first birthday after your loss.
The first holidays you celebrate after your loss.

It may not dawn on you why facing a particular event seems so hard until you realize this is a first. You may try to delay and avoid some of these firsts. They can be difficult, but then once they are passed, the second is easier, then the third and forth. Face them knowing that you only have to do the first one time.

The first holidays may be especially challenging. I began dreading my first Mother's Day several weeks before. I have two sons and, of course, have always enjoyed the cards and gifts I receive from them. But, the fact that my third son was not there was looming large for me on the horizon. When the day came, I found my solution. I visited Isaac's grave and left flowers. Spending time visiting Isaac and telling him how much I missed him helped me make that motherly connection I was needing that day. I continued to visit his grave every Mother's Day for several years.

For other holiday observances that year we included Isaac by making special silk flower arrangements for his grave and making a family outing to the cemetery part of the day's events. I noticed that other families at the cemetery left toys or balloons at their baby's graves.

If you do not have a grave to visit, you might pick a spot where you can go and feel at peace. There may be a nearby lake or park where you can go, or a special tree or bench in your yard. I know a lady who placed her baby's urn on a special shelf in her bedroom and that was her place. Find a place for yourself and visit when you feel the need.

Christmas was our biggest challenge as far as holidays that first year. I think it would have been challenging anyway but the fact that our son died on Christmas Day the year before made it even more so. We considered doing something different that year, perhaps going to a vacation spot instead of visiting family. We felt a need for a change in our traditions but were not sure what that change should be. It was important that we honor Isaac but also provide a good Christmas for our other sons.

We ended up deciding to keep most of our traditions but made some small changes. That year we started a Christmas village. It is nothing very fancy, we started with just a couple of buildings and let my sons pick out some accessories. We continue our village to this day. Each year we will pick out another building and more accessories or people. The village has become a major part of our holiday tradition. It has more funky looking cars than Christmas villages normally would, but my sons have had a lot of fun with it through the years. I think of Isaac every year when we pull the village out and what fun he would have had with his brothers setting up that village and fighting over where to put Santa Claus.

Another tradition was started by my father that year at our large family gathering. We light a candle in Isaac's memory every year before we open gifts. We stop and remind ourselves how old he would be on that day and imagine what he would be like. In the years since, we have also started including other family members who have died in our candle lighting ceremony. It is a very meaningful part of our Christmas tradition.

You may want to find your own traditions for the holidays that are most difficult for you. You also need to feel free to change old traditions if they no longer work for you. Discover what helps you make the day meaningful. It does not have to be anything large or earth shattering, just find what works for you.

Anniversary

The first anniversary of your loss will probably bring a new wave of grief. You may begin dreading the day a few weeks ahead. You may not even realize it at first but will notice that you are perhaps feeling irritable or unsettled.

I did not realize that the first anniversary was weighing on my mind until a group I was a part of expected me to do the holiday shopping for a needy family. I had done it in years past and they naturally assumed I would do it again that year. It wasn't until I nearly bit my friend's head off, when she mentioned the shopping, that I realized how much I was dreading that first anniversary.

The actual day will likely not be as hard as the anticipation of it. Once the day arrives, it is not nearly as difficult as you expect. It may help to plan for the day. Perhaps have a special family gathering and light a candle, visit the grave or your special spot. Honor and remember your child that day, and honor yourself that you survived the year.

Reaching that one year mark does not mean you have completed your journey and will no longer be in grief. But it will have special significance for you. Do something to commemorate the day.

The God Question

As you struggle to put one foot in front of the other you may find yourself running into the same brick wall. Vickie said:

> *I do remember trying to pray. I asked and wondered "Why me" and "What did I do to deserve this" and "Why couldn't you have given me a child to love?" And reminding God that there were people that mistreat and abuse children. Why was I singled out?*

I realize this section may not speak to everyone. If that is the case for you, then just skip ahead. I do want to address this issue though, because this was definitely something I had to work through in my grief experience. If you do read on in this section, I want to stress to you that I am not a theologian and am not trying to be. These are my answers to my struggles and you may not reach the same conclusions. My hope is that it will be food for thought and you will find the answers that work for you.

There tends to be a bit of the magical in our beliefs about God. Religion can be a tricky thing, we know in our heads that bad things happen in the world to good and bad people alike but we don't really know that in our guts. We hear the stories of how someone was supposed to be on a plane that crashed but they, for some reason, missed the flight. What do we do? We immediately exclaim how it is a miracle that God rescued this good person. We hear stories on the news about people who narrowly escaped death and how often do we hear them say that God had protected them?

We don't usually stop to consider that most of the people that die in plane crashes are good people. Most of the thousands and thousands of funerals which are performed each year are for good people. But somehow we still believe that God won't let anything bad happen to us. Somehow we feel immune.

I have to admit that I was wrapped up in this kind of thinking. My son, Zach, was born eight weeks premature. Our fears when he was born soon turned to joy when it turned out that he was on oxygen for less than 24 hours, he was healthy and strong and spent less than a week in the hospital. When we found out he had had a knot in his umbilical cord, we rejoiced that God had brought him into the world early before that knot had tightened and cut off his oxygen supply. I truly believed God had reached out His hand to protect my son. I believed that with all my heart for six years.

Then Isaac died.

It challenged my faith in ways that nothing had before. If I believed God had reached out and saved one son, then I had to believe He had chosen not to save the other.

You may have a similar struggle, or you may be wondering why God singled you out, as Vicki did. You may even believe that you do deserve this, that this is punishment.

I believe a lot of our difficulties when we face tragedy come down to one word, control. So much of our lives are spent trying to control the world around us.

I used to try to control my children. I thought that was what a good parent did. In the same way, my religious life was wrapped up in control. God was trying to control me and I was trying to control Him through my prayers.

Whether you are questioning why God singled you out, or you believe He is punishing you for past sins, you see God as controlling the events in your life.

What helped me was learning to leave the word control behind. I became a far better parent when I started relating to my sons as people due my respect and trust. And when I started leaving control out of my dealings with God, everything changed. I was no longer caught up in trying to be good enough or fretting over every little transgression and worried about punishment. I found a new word. I found the word acceptance.

I found acceptance that good and bad things happen to both those who deserve it and those who don't. Acceptance that I may not be perfect, but I don't have to be. Acceptance that I cannot control the world around me. I found acceptance that both good and bad will come my way and there are just too many things I cannot control. I found acceptance that life is sometimes hard but it is also sometimes filled with more joy than I could imagine.

My path to giving up control and learning acceptance was not easy. I spent many years struggling with this question. You may have your own struggles within your own belief system. All I can say is my struggles brought me to a new understanding in my beliefs about God and religion. I lost something through the struggle but ended up with something much deeper to take its place. I lost the magical idea that I can be a good person and pray and somehow be protected. But in the process I gained an understanding that my spiritual life is a relationship that goes beyond events that are happening in my life. I found acceptance that Isaac's death did not mean I was being singled out by God, nor was I being punished. It was one of the tragedies that happen in life to good and bad people alike.

That is my answer. You will have to find your own.

Your Relationship

Every couple will find themselves in a struggle of how to cope with a loss, both as a couple and as individuals. In some ways this type of loss causes an extra strain on the relationship.

After a tragic event you naturally seek closeness and security with your loved ones. One element of that is intimacy with your mate. However, added into the mix of this tragic event is that the very act of making love to one another is also how your child was conceived. On the one hand you are longing for that ultimate closeness but, on the other hand, it brings up all your feelings of loss.

Openness, honesty, and patience are key here. Each couple has to find their own way to navigate through troubled times. It may help to realize that men and women tend to grieve differently and, beyond that, each individual grieves in their own way.

Some differences between men and women in grief are easy to see. Women feel more freedom to cry in front of others, while men generally do not like to let anyone see them do so. Women are often more able to talk about their feelings openly, while men tend to be more private or may express themselves in more physical ways with fewer words. But there are other differences at this time that are not as easy to see.

Men tend to feel a great helplessness in their ability to take care of their family. This is one time when there is nothing they can do to protect them. They feel a loss of control that is not easy to face. There is also a feeling of being ill qualified to know how to help their mate and they may be frightened or unsure of themselves. They may be afraid that they will say or do the wrong thing. They may be angry about the whole situation.

I know one man who felt so much anger and frustration that he wanted to destroy something. He went out to his front lawn to trim his tree, but instead ended up cutting the whole tree down. It may have been bad for his landscaping, but I am glad he found a way to vent some of his frustration.

Men may also desire normalcy and will return to their normal routine quicker. They may see this as fulfilling their responsibility to take care of the family, or it may be a longing for things to return to where they were before the loss. It may lend them a feeling of being in control of their world. For whatever reason, men do tend to get back into all their normal activities faster than women after a loss.

There is nothing wrong with returning to their routine. However they need to keep in mind that their spouse may be feeling left behind. I remember a couple of months after Isaac died my husband walked in after work one day and said that he had had time to think about it and grieve and that he was now "over it." I don't remember what I said but I do remember what I felt—lonely. That was the loneliest day of my entire life. That meant that I was now the only one grieving over Isaac. I don't believe my husband had any intention of hurting me with his statement but I truly felt abandoned.

Men also face the expectations of society. After this type of loss people will be supportive but they will generally ask the husband about his wife, "How is she doing?" All the focus is on the woman whereas few people ask the man how he is doing. The hidden message is that this should not be hard on the man, he should only feel a small bit of sadness and he should be strong for his wife. What is lacking is the support for him. Instead of feeling supported, he may feel pressured to act as if he is doing fine, to put on a good face. That can be a difficult burden to bear.

Couples have to find their own way through their grief, both as individuals and as a couple. It can be a challenge. Men and women both need to find someone they can talk to about their grief. But, they should be aware that since they are both struggling with their own grief, they may not be able to hold each other up. Rely on each other but also rely on friends. Do not expect your partner to be able to handle the full load of their own grief and yours too.

A major event in your lives such as this changes your relationship and in some ways you have to rebuild it. Understand that rebuilding it takes time and effort. As a couple, you need to talk to each other and find ways to show each other how you feel. Things left unsaid now can fester and cause a wall to come between you. Be careful of each other's feelings in how you speak but find ways to broach any subject that is causing a distance between you. Acts of kindness can also speak volumes in how you feel about each other. Acts of kindness can be as simple as taking care of one of the chores for the other person or leaving a card on their pillow with a note of how much you appreciate them.

Talk, be patient, be kind.

Other Children in the Home

It is natural if you have other children in the home to be concerned about how they will handle this loss. For the most part, they will be more concerned that their parents are upset. The main thing they will need is reassurance that things will be okay.

My sons were ages six and eight when we lost Isaac and they found a unique way of expressing their feelings. We went to my parents' home for a few days after the funeral. My sons went down to the playroom in the basement. Normally, adults were not invited to join them down there. But, on this occasion, we were asked to come downstairs. My sons had created a series of stations around the basement using drawings, toys and clothes. The stations depicted a whole life for Isaac. Each station was set up to reflect something about him and what they imagined for their little brother.

I was very touched by what my sons had done and I think it helped them in many ways. They were able to participate in the whole grief experience of the family, they were able to show my husband and I how deeply they cared and I also felt that it expressed some of their insecurity at that time. What my sons were doing was working through and experiencing their feelings through play which is typical of children of that age.

There are many factors that affect how your children will handle this loss. Their age and their involvement in preparations for the expected baby will play a part. But watching how you, their parents, deal with the loss will play the largest part.

Do not feel that you have to be strong and stoical in their presence. It is okay for your children to see you cry. It is important to explain to them that you are upset, but you are not upset with them. Tell them you are sad and that it will take some time to get over being sad, but that you will be okay and they will be okay.

It is alright to talk about the baby with them. Children often wonder if they caused the baby to die, reassure them they did not. Answer their questions openly and honestly. You don't have to give a lot of details; simple, honest answers work best. If you feel your child's response seems extreme, you may want to seek advice from a professional. However, most children just need to feel secure and loved. Give them that and you will all be okay.

Another Child

There is a great deal of variance on when couples want to try another pregnancy, or if they try again at all.

The first step to take is to talk to your doctor to discuss any physical issues. If your physician advices you to wait before your next pregnancy, I would strongly encourage you to follow their advice. Ignoring it could pose a danger to you or to your next child.

Beyond physical concerns are other issues to consider such as when you are ready emotionally. It is not a matter of being totally over grief before having another baby, but there is a sense of the right time. You will have to determine when the time is right for you. Also be aware of the reactions of your family and friends.

I met a wonderful young lady named Julie at a Compassionate Friends convention in Oklahoma City. She told me she had not told her friends why she had come to Oklahoma City, so I asked her to tell me her story. Julie had lost her newborn son. She became pregnant again within just a couple of months, earlier than she had planned. She now has a beautiful little girl whom she loves dearly. However, her family and friends do not understand why she still grieves for her first child. They seem to think that since she now has a baby, her grief should be over. They do not understand that one baby can not replace another. Julie's joy for her daughter does not eliminate the grief for her son. The pressure on Julie to get over her grief and move on became so great that she stopped talking about it. She became locked in a prison of silence and now found herself sneaking off to a Compassionate Friends convention where she knew she would have somewhere to share her story and grieve openly.

The decision whether or not to become pregnant again is unique to each individual and situation: your age, family situation, financial situation, the circumstances of your loss, or where you are in the grief process are all factors. You might ask yourself if the loss you suffered still consumes you? Are all your thoughts about the baby you lost? Are you becoming obsessed with the idea of becoming pregnant again? If so, this may mean you are not ready. Are you at a point where thinking about the loss still tears you apart, or are you at a point where you feel happiness again and can laugh and enjoy other people again? Don't rush in believing that another pregnancy will take your grief away. The only way to get through grief is to grieve and another pregnancy too soon will not make it easier.

Laughing and Living Again

They say that laughter is the best medicine. However, for a few months after Isaac died I felt a pang of guilt every time I laughed. I felt neglectful whenever I realized that an hour had passed and I had not thought of Isaac. It was as if laughing meant I wasn't showing the proper amount of love and respect for Isaac.

Doing anything "fun" was difficult for a while. My husband wanted to go to a movie a couple of weeks after Isaac died. I did not have any desire to go. I was too sad and depressed and in too much pain. However, he talked me into going. I was miserable but perhaps it was helpful for him and our sons to do something fun again. At the time I did not think I would ever be able to enjoy movies or any of the other fun things we used to do. I just could not imagine ever caring about those things again.

Getting back in to life is hard and it does take time. It is so hard because it is a process of letting go, of realizing it is possible to honor your child and feel joy at the same time.

Eventually, I was able to let go, a little at a time. The day came when I was able to laugh and not feel guilty. The day came when I did not think of Isaac for a long stretch of time, and I was comfortable with that. The day came when I was able to put the mementos of Isaac in a plastic tub in my closet and not need to keep them before me at all times. It did not happen suddenly but, little by little, I made progress.

Am I done grieving? I don't know that you are ever really done. I came through the intense pain of those early months, and I found a way to live with the grief. I think of Isaac from time to time throughout the year. I keep up with the years, I know how old he would be. I occasionally wonder what he would be like at this age and what a terror he would be to his older bothers. I sometimes wonder how life would be different if he had lived. But, Isaac is no longer the entire focus of my life, I am more than a grieving parent. I can now laugh and live again and while the grief no longer consumes me, it is still a part of me.

You will find your own way back to laughing and living again. It is not something that can be rushed, but, little by little, you will make progress. For now, grieve. But do so in the knowledge that you will survive it and your grief will one day be a part of you, but not all of you.

I wish to close this letter with my best wishes to you and your family and my heartfelt desire to make your journey through grief a little easier.

Love,
Kathy

About the Author

Kathy Manning Burns

Kathy is a Vice President of In-Sight Books, graphic designer for In-Sight Institute and an In-Sight Institute Certified Funeral Celebrant. She is a volunteer in the Parents Responding to Infant Death Experience (PRIDE) program at a local hospital and completed RTS Bereavement Training in early pregnancy loss, stillbirth, & newborn death in 2009. She has two adult sons and has written this book in memory of her third son, Isaac.

Resources

Other Resources From In-Sight Books

Don't Take My Grief Away From Me by Doug Manning
Thoughts for the Lonely Nights by Doug Manning (book or CD)
The Journey of Grief DVD by Doug Manning
I Know Someone Who Died coloring book by Connie Manning
Comfort Cards
Footprints and other Lapel Pins

For a catalog or ordering information:

In-Sight Books, Inc.
800.658.9262 or 405.810.9501
www.InSightBooks.com
OrdersAndInfo@InSightBooks.com

Visit TheCareCommunity.com for Doug Manning's blogs on Grief and Elder Care